Anna Karczewska Slowikowska

Black Rose and African Violets

Limited Special Edition. No. 24 of 25 Paperbacks

Anna Karczewska Slowikowska is a retired Chartered Psychologist. For over 30 years, she worked in the voluntary, statutory and private sectors, during which time she had a number of articles published. Her interest in her mother's wartime experiences developed from a curiosity to learn more about her and to research her familial past. The tranquillity of her home in the beautiful Scottish Borders town of Melrose helped her write of her mother's disturbing background.

Anna has two children, Beatrix and Alexander, and three granddaughters, and each year commutes between Australia and Scotland.

Time is also spent in her architectural award-winning home, playing tennis and badminton. Anna has recently become a member of Probus and volunteers with Talking Newspapers for the blind.

To the memory of my mother, Ludomira Gwizdalska.

I dedicate this story to my dear family; childhood friend, Nina Popowska, an inheritor of the past; and to my three granddaughters, Hannah, Amber and Yve, inheritors of the future.

Anna Karczewska Slowikowska

Black Rose and African Violets

Austin Macauley Publishers™
London • Cambridge • New York • Sharjah

A CIP catalogue record for this title is available from the British Library.

ISBN 9781528905282 (Paperback)
ISBN 9781528905299 (E-Book)

www.austinmacauley.com

First Published (2019)
Austin Macauley Publishers Ltd
25 Canada Square
Canary Wharf
London
E14 5LQ

I have received encouragement from members of my family; my brother, Janusz Karczewski Slowikowski; niece, Zoe Carletides; daughter, Beatrix Tomlin, for initially reading the first draft. To my son, Alex, for his enduring patience in coming to my aid with technical computer difficulties.

To my friend Louise Nicol-Smith for her honest comments and suggestions.

To Nick Elliott, without whom, this book would not have reached publication; his help and support enabled me to continue. To Professor Norman Davies, whose initial comments made the project not just an idea, but a possibility.

I am grateful to the Scottish Borders Scribblers with their sharing of ideas and suggestions and for taking me into their fold.

Special thanks to Helen Bleck, my editor, whose patience and expertise I could not have done without.

Table of Contents

Foreword

This is a story of my mother, Ludomira Gwizdalska, a refugee from Poland. She was the youngest daughter of a Polish army officer who, she informed me, was shot early on in the Second World War in 1939. At the outbreak of war between Nazi Germany and Poland in 1939, my mother, aged 18, was a nurse in the Warsaw general hospital. After its capture by the Nazis, Mother was sent to Auschwitz and then Belsen concentration camp. One night, in Belsen together with another prisoner, she hid under dead bodies that were waiting to be disposed of in quicklime. The following morning, she made her escape but was shot in the shoulder during the attempt and recaptured. Sometime after this she was sent to Siberia for hard labour.

It was by asking questions and much research that I learned of the rape and ill-treatment she underwent at the hands of both Nazi and Russian soldiers at various times of her capture.

It has not been an easy process either discovering or writing her story, and at times I have wondered whether Mother would have wanted me to put her life onto paper. I could choose to ignore it, but if I did that then what Mother endured would be unacknowledged. And I have a fundamental curiosity about my familial past; an urge to know and touch on the geography of my parents' pre-war lives; to explore the 'what if' questions…

***

I tell Mother's story and especially my relationship with her through my own reflective journey: an unfolding of events firstly growing up in post-war Britain as a young girl of nine protected by a kind and loving mother; then through my adult eyes, as a mother and grandmother myself, in the knowledge that, despite my doubts as to whether she would want me to commit her story to paper. I believe it should be told—as one of the many people who went through the horrors of the Second World War in Poland. It has taken me almost a lifetime to uncover what happened to her, mainly due to her own silence, the very indirect revelations I received from her and others, and the scars I sensed and saw, which prevented me from asking more questions. In doing so, I believe the psychological and moral dilemmas that people experienced at times of persecution and war can affect the generations that follow, and my discoveries have led me to understand why many survivors of wartime Poland under the Nazi regime kept a veil of silence, whether through shame, or trauma or in trying to forget what they had witnessed and experienced, as in my mother's case.

Some names have been changed to protect individuals.

***

Chapter 1
The Journey

Our story begins with a train journey my mother and I took when I was nine years old. The scene is post-war Britain, the year 1956. I remember I was wearing a dusty-pink lightweight tweed suit, pleated skirt and fitted jacket with white nylon blouse. I wanted to look my best. My hair was tied back in a ponytail with a white ribbon. It had grown since I had left Heathfield, where we were returning, and I wanted to show how grownup I was.

We sat opposite one another, gazing out of the carriage window. It must have been late spring and everything looked green as we passed through the Sussex countryside.

The wooden panels of the carriage gleamed in the sunlight; the glass frame above Mother's head contained a poster of children playing at the seaside in bright, playful colours. The carriage was empty and no travellers drifted past in the corridor. I remember the sound of the train's piercing whistle as we stopped at stations on the way, together with the smell of steam gushing through the window. I glanced occasionally at Mother; we were both isolated in our own thoughts. I, in anticipation of reclaiming books and belongings that I felt were rightfully mine, especially a Polish book entitled *Pan Twardowski*—about a man who sold his soul to the Devil in exchange for magical powers—a child's version of the story that I had begun to cherish. It just seemed to me that the characters in the book resonated with a special meaning, revealing a culture felt but not fully experienced, the pictures vivid with colour and larger-than-life characters from a land I wanted to get to know. Although I was always self-confident, I knew I was different from other children prior to attending Heathfield; my name, I had a different accent. I looked the same as other children, maybe it was the way I conducted myself, a little aloof, and happy in my own company.

The train made a lovely rickety-track noise as it glided over the rails, our bodies moving back and forth with the motion. I remember thinking I had been on one of these journeys before, passing rolling countryside and undulating hills, but could not recall exactly when or where. Mother made no sound, although her face wore a look of contentment and anticipation, all at the same time. It never crossed my mind to ask, 'What are you thinking?' I just saw her beautiful face and hair brushed back, her black earrings and smart black suit fitted at the waist. She always looked elegant to me, in my early years of growing up. We both sat upright, our backs straight, I on the edge of my seat wanting to see all that passed. I recall how we spoke very little, yet I felt we were very connected on that journey into Sussex.

Chapter 2
Virgo Fidelis

I first noticed I was a little different from other children at Virgo Fidelis convent school, in Upper Norwood: an independent school for girls, and where I boarded prior to attending St Catherine's House in Heathfield Sussex. My name for a start, where had I come from—difficult for me to explain to others who asked. My brother Janusz also boarded, as they took boys in the infant section of the school. The fact that I did not live at home most of the time seemed of little consequence as other girls also boarded. The school was a short distance away from the large Victorian house Mother rented from Joan Gregory and her mother. Aunty Joan as we called her seemed a permanent figure in our lives; it was she who escorted us and Mother to purchase my school uniform, all of navy and light blue with name tags sowed in every part of our clothing; Anna Maria Karczewska and Janusz David Martin Karczewski respectively.

I was between six and seven years old when I attended Virgo Fidelis. My memory prior to that time is like pieces of a jigsaw all individually placed, but not connected and with some pieces missing. Many of the photographs I have, show Janusz as a baby and myself as a toddler, happy and smiling, well cared for in a respectable pre-war house with lattice windows and gardens laid to lawn, a wedding ring visible on Mother's right hand. In those pictures Mother looks pensive and thin, yet stood proud and erect. Some of the photographs are of nuns, of whom Mother had fond memories. Mother obtained work in convents as a domestic servant or as a nursery assistant during my formative years. I once asked her who the nuns were and she named them all, especially mentioned Sister Alberta, although she never said when or where they had met. So it did not seem strange to me to find myself boarding in a convent full of nuns lined up looking like the black and white sweets from a packet of liquorish all-sorts. The nuns seemed very stern except for Mother Superior, whenever I did see her she was smiling. How Mother and Aunty Joan met I am unsure. They did remain friends for some time and I continued that friendship with Aunty Joan until Joan's death in the late eighties. I was not even aware of how Mother came to be in the UK at that time; however, realising that Mother spoke differently, sometimes in Polish and then English with a broken accent created an air of intrigue. There was no husband, just the three of us.

Apart from Aunty Joan, Mother made friends with a work colleague, a lady called Helen. Helen was Scottish and became my godmother, and would take Janusz and me on trips to the zoo and boat trips on the Thames. So Mother had the friendship of women who were there to help her.

The rented flat in Auntie Joan's house was very homely, with doors leading out into the garden, where Janusz and I would play when home from school. Joan's mother was a stern woman with white hair and a frail frame who had lost her husband in the First World War. Auntie Joan would never talk about her father: again, such silence. She would, however, make up little bags of sweets for us and throw them out of the window when we were playing in the garden. I distinctly remember cuddling up to Mother on the chintz sofa in front of a huge open fire, where she read me stories from a Victorian book about the bread fairies, the flower fairies and all manner of other fairies. These are special memories. They were read in English interspersed with Polish, I don't think she was reading the words but describing what she saw on the page. When Queen Elizabeth II celebrated her coronation, we sat upstairs with a number of other people to watch the coronation on a large wooden television set with a rather small screen. Sandwiches were handed around and a toast raised to the young Queen. I knew we were not part of the family yet they made us feel welcomed. At this time I sensed Mother was happy. She would wear a perfume called Black Rose by Goya, along with a ruby ring and a beautiful cameo brooch. I once wore the brooch in my teens, when wanting to look all grown up. Needless to say I lost that brooch and felt very bad about that. I have since tried to make up for it by collecting various cameos of differing shapes and sizes, and hope to pass these on. Mother wore a delicate gold crucifix and on each corner of the central crucifix was another delicately placed cross. I never saw her without it. I did ask her where it came from; there was no direct reply, just her hand placed gently on it.

Mother's way was always to try to make a home comfortable. My bedroom was once where the coal was kept and when returning home from boarding school one weekend, I found it brightly painted in a soft green. Sometimes I was allowed to sleep in her bed. I don't ever remember birthdays, except one weekend while at Virgo Fidelis there was a big party in the refectory. Apparently it was my eighth birthday and Mother had sent a big cake, although name days were usually more celebrated than actual birth dates in the Polish tradition. It was a surprise to me that it was my birthday.

It was at Virgo Fidelis that I made my first Holy Communion. I remember distinctly being taken to a dressmaker's by Mother and Auntie Joan to have a white dress made for me. Mother wanted me to have a headband made of Lilly of the Valley, which was kept in water overnight to keep it fresh. The nuns were not pleased, but it seemed Mother always got her own way. I am told, Lilly of the Valley symbolises a return to happiness; maybe Mother was trying to bring back happiness from what she had lost!

I still have my reports from the school, where I was a promising pupil, although I am not sure whether I was particularly liked by the nuns. One evening after we had finished supper, I was made to stand on a chair in front of the whole school. I was made an example of how not to wear a school uniform. My collars were all chewed and my tunic came back from the laundry covered with food which I had not liked and had placed in my pockets. I particularly disliked blancmange, and also the overcooked crimpled edges of fried eggs. It was a very harsh punishment in front of the whole school. *Jane Eyre* comes to mind. I always thought of myself as happy and confident, yet there appear times when I must have been highly anxious and chewed the corners of my collar looking a little unkempt. I always had to remember there were indoor shoes and outdoor shoes.

I had some good friends at the school and one in particular, called Sozia and her older sister, Danuta, whose mother was Polish; however, they did not have a very Polish-sounding name. Their mother had also been in the camps although I did not know that at the time. I went to stay with their family in Tunbridge Wells during the holidays. They had a coffee shop in the Pantiles. The family lived above the shop and the smell of coffee drifted up into the house. I can visualise the scene and smell the coffee as I write.

I later heard that Sozia was also not popular with the nuns and now suffers as a second-generation survivor of parents who were sent to the concentration camps. She cried and was unhappy; I felt drawn towards her. When I was starting work on this book, I contacted Danuta. She has a good life and her daughter also manages to get on with her life with little adverse effects from her family's experiences during the war. We never did meet up, but we did remain in contact via e-mail and talked about our time at Virgo Fidelis. After a while, she wrote to say she no longer wanted to dwell on the past, probably because it was too painful and she felt her life was going backwards instead of moving on. I was unable to speak to her sister Sozia, as I was told she had suffered psychologically and did not want to be reminded of the past. Her relationship with her mother was fraught with anguish. Danuta, on the other hand, had managed to escape from all that and had moved on. We concluded that despite the horrendous lives our mothers experienced, we, meaning she and I, turned out surprisingly unscathed.

***

Holiday times were carefree and happy. We would venture out into the Sussex countryside and play amongst the hay and paddle our feet in streams. To this day I love the colour of freshly harvested hay, and much prefer the countryside to living in a town. I mention all this as it shows how hard Mother must have worked to give Janusz and me a happy life and provide for our schooling. I somehow thought Auntie Joan paid my school fees but no, she told me later on in my life that Mother managed it all. Mother was trying to make a new life for herself, as most people had to after the war, but perhaps her experiences helped her get a sympathetic ear when it came to helping her children. I have sometimes wondered whether she managed to persuade Mother Superior to give us free places at school.

In London, Mother had access to a wider Polish community and made friends with other Polish people; Janusz and I would play hide and seek with the children while the grown-ups talked over cups of tea. It seems we have an idealised view of childhood when growing up; reflecting on hard times and trauma is the privilege of a mature brain.

I wonder now how Mother managed to be so caring and achieve so much on her own while remaining so elegant and poised during those early years. She always looked smart with well-tailored clothes and her hair short and tied back with combs. I sensed there was a strict and stern side to her when dealing with others, but she never had a harsh word for Janusz or me. Mother was never quiet in political debates and had her own opinions. She was at times philosophical, informing me; for instance, that men and women had equal rights: sometimes the man was the head and the woman the neck and vice versa, neither could do without the other. Maybe this was an old Polish saying.

At age eight, Mother decided to send Janusz and me to St Catherine's House at Heathfield in Sussex, a boarding school especially for refugee Polish children. Why or who made that decision is difficult to know. Her private life was hidden from us as we were at school most of the time. I distinctly remember the red leather briefcase filled with numerous letters in Par

Avion envelopes. These envelopes appeared periodically, and I would often see Mother reading them, folding them neatly, tying them up with the ribbon and placing them back in the red case.

Chapter 3
Heathfield

Heathfield was, and is, a delightful market town in Sussex, home of the Spring Cuckoo Fair and the railway known as the Cuckoo Line serving the Sussex communities, though it is now no longer in use. Tradition goes that at the fair, held in spring each year, a lady would release a cuckoo from a basket, supposedly the first cuckoo of spring.

I can't remember how we got to St Catherine's house after we alighted at Heathfield station, that day Mother and I returned to retrieve my belongings. I don't remember how we got back to the railway station after the visit, only the disappointment felt at not achieving my objective.

St Catherine's house—a large Edwardian house set in its own grounds and run by a small skeleton staff, felt deeply familiar as we entered; the smell was still the same and to this day I sometimes sense that same smell of buckwheat and chicken stock lingering in the background, especially at Christmas and Easter time. It takes me back to this place of my childhood. The garden at the back of the house was my favourite spot, together with the large sitting room with its comfortable chairs, which was mainly for visitors. One entered the garden through large French windows and down concrete steps. A small kitchen garden was to the left side of the property, where neat rows of flowers and vegetables grew. Brown hens wandered in the garden. Nothing had changed from how I remembered it.

Having been born in Great Britain, with English my first language, it was here at Heathfield that I first learned about and inhabited another culture. Up and till that time I was aware that my mother had an unusual accent when she spoke; now everyone around me had that same accent. I had yet to learn of what horrors she had witnessed and been through. She was just my mother whom I loved.

The children who had remained at St Catherine's greeted me with enthusiasm. I remember greeting them fondly after my two years' absence. They did not ask me where I had been or why I had left, they had just accepted that one day I was no longer there. As far as I was concerned, I had come back for my books and toys, they were part of my childhood, a reminder of my two and a half years as a boarder there: my dolls, the easel Mother had bought me one Christmas—not a great deal, but enough to matter to me. It was the first time I had a sense of holding onto something. No *Pan Twardowski* could be found.

"Never mind," Mother said. "I'll get you another."

Not the same, I thought.

After I'd played and talked enough with the children, Pania Archichewska, matron and administrator of the home, a formidable woman, looked me over with approval. I never knew what she and Mother talked about when Mother visited, probably finances or what was to become of me. I looked at her with some trepidation. Pania Archichewska was the wife of Thomasz Archichewski, the last prime minister of the wartime Polish government-in-exile. He appeared a kind gentleman with white hair and a goatee beard. I learned many years later that his role after the war was to protect the children of Poland and to enable them to carry on the Polish culture. 'They are our future,' he once wrote. His aim was to preserve the Polish language and its culture. All the children at St Catherine's had Polish parents, some of whom were still looking for one or other member of their family. For Pan Archichewski, accommodating to a British culture was one thing; assimilating whilst holding onto one's Polish past was quite another. According to him, it was as important as ever now for us Poles to hold onto our Polish roots. We learnt to speak Polish and to dance and sing Polish songs, and watched films about the Polish Air Force and their historic contribution to the Battle of Britain.

Many years later, as an adult standing in St Peter's Square, I heard the then Polish Pope John Paul II echo the same sentiment. In his Easter message to the world, in seven languages (including Polish), he said, 'Do not forget where you came from. Remember your roots.' I felt at the time he was speaking directly to me as I expect everyone else who stood in the square thought he was speaking to each person individually. As a pupil at Heathfield, we watched the television adaptation of Robert Louis Stevenson's *Kidnapped* on a small Bakelite screen to mark the connection between Scotland and Poland., Charles Edward Stuart, better known as Bonnie Prince Charlie, was half Polish. His mother was Maria Clementina Sobieska, the granddaughter of the Polish king, Jan Sobieski III. I am very grateful for that experience, as it has instilled in me a pride that lingers in my heart today and led me to study further historical connections between the two countries that go back to the 1500s. There was no direct teaching of history, just the realisation of how Polish airmen had fought in the battle of Britain and how proud we were to be of our Polish heritage and culture.

I was a good dancer and tended to play the boy's role in the 'Krakowiak' and the 'Polonaise', a Polish national dance, which we learned at Heathfield. I felt good dancing. At Heathfield, they informed Mother of my dancing ability, Mother replied I could go and learn ballet, that her own mother had been a classical ballet dancer in Lithuania, how she would have achieved this I don't know. I always had the feeling she wanted the best for me.

After I left Heathfield, I remember thinking about the Christmases we had there. The long meals from eight in the evening when the first star appeared on Christmas Eve, the various courses and especially the crisp orange peel covered in sugar, and the giving-out of presents later in the evening—only one would be given out on Christmas Eve. It was usually then that the parents arrived. Some came for the meal but Mother never made it in time and I remember waiting for her to come as they were handing out the presents. Sadness would fall over me when I did not see her, but I always knew in my heart that she would come. At that age, it never crossed my mind to wonder how she got to Heathfield, whether by car or by train. I can remember feeling so proud and happy when she did arrive. To me, she looked so lovely, more beautiful than ever. Once, I opened my present to find it was a large easel with a blackboard, how it got there I have no idea. That was the blackboard that I had wanted to retrieve on my return visit to Heathfield together with my books.

At Heathfield, I enjoyed the countryside; the Sunday walk to church; attending Maynard's Green infant school a short bus ride away; learning to read from *John Bull* magazines as well as the Janet and John books; the school dinners—I can still remember the mashed potatoes, the creamiest I have ever tasted. Buying Spangles in the village shop while waiting for the bus was a particular treat. I liked Spangles because they lasted so long and I could place my tongue in the square centre of the sweet.

Janusz, my brother, three years younger than me, was always getting into mischief. The boys slept in a different dormitory and I would often go and see if he was all right and not in some sort of detention or having to polish shoes as a punishment for some misdeed or other.

I was aware of there being a different neighbourhood, with children who went to day school and returned home to their parents every afternoon. I wondered, looking out of the dormitory window to the house opposite, how it must feel to live in a house with parents and come home every day. It never occurred to me to think of the life Mother had while she was living miles away in London while I boarded at Heathfield.

I think of Heathfield as my Polish childhood. I have often reflected on the children there and the parents who came to visit and wondered whatever happened to them. One mother, who visited her daughter at Heathfield, worked in the Mars factory in Slough and brought with her Mars bars without the wrappings to share among us. After St Catherine's closed in the late fifties, my friend Nina went on to Pittsford, a private school for girls in Northampton. The boys moved on to Fawley Court in Herefordshire, or back to their parents once they were settled into the community. My brother and I went to live in South London with Mother, where we continued Polish lessons at Saturday school.

Round about the time I was leaving Heathfield, I remember on a visit home going to the Polish Embassy in Kensington, again in my best dusty-pink tweed suit, I had not grown a great deal. I sat outside an office on an upright chair while Mother went in to see the Polish ambassador. After a while, I was invited in. “This is my daughter, Anya,” she introduced me. He looked at me and smiled. We had some polite conversation, though I can’t remember what was said. I only remember the look. I later wondered whether he had any connection to my father. Janusz had said he also had a similar visit and remembered meeting him. Mother was contemplating getting married, and permission would have been required especially in relation to her first marriage. If her first husband was still alive, then she would be committing an act of bigamy. It has been difficult to obtain information regarding her time in Russia, and in recognising the various camps in the Soviet Gulag.

There were many visits to various official offices, and at one point I was informed by one of the staff at Heathfield that I would be going on a journey—though where to, I was not told. For some reason Australia comes to mind. Many children were being sent to convents in Australia in the nineteen fifties, with dire consequences for some of them. Mother was courting with my stepfather at this time, and I later wondered whether he was not ready to take on both Janusz and me. This was reinforced when I once asked Mother why she looked so pensive prior to entering the church on her wedding day. “I was thinking of you both and what was to become of you,” she said. It was while we were in Heathfield that Mother got married. However, we did end up all living together. I and my brother Janusz were adopted in 1959, two years after their marriage and given the name Slowikowska and Slowikowski respectively. I found it difficult to give up my previous surname, all my school clothes were labeled Karczewska and everyone knew me as Karczewska, so Janusz and I decided to have both.

28 Ennersdale Road, Hither Green, South London was the house we moved to where my stepfather had a flat, an upstairs flat in a terraced Edwardian house. I had little or no concrete knowledge of Mother's past. She never talked about her parents or even about Poland, and certainly not about the war. The only information I had about my Polish heritage was what I had learned at Heathfield. It now dawned on me that yes, although being born in the UK my mother wasn't and there had been a terrible war and somehow my mother had been a part of it. It did not seem to matter then, all my needs were met. I now had some knowledge of Poland and the war, but it was only as a result of my research long after she had died that I learned more of Mother's time in the concentration camps in Poland and from information released to me by the Home Office including her army and medical records. Of course, I was aware of something terrible had happened, there had been a war between Germany and the United Kingdom but not how Poland fitted into all this. It was a later realisation that Mother was protecting us from the horror of what happened.

Many people were looking for their relatives after the war and renewing contact with those who were found. While researching this story and searching through many archives, I often came across the names of grandparents of my former school friends, people who had died in the death camps, or through other unforeseen circumstances. Did my friends ever know? I wondered about the parents of the children at Heathfield who came to visit, and what their parents' lives were like during the war years. Did they know my mother during that time?

Many years later, my childhood friend Nina wondered about the fate of St Catherine's. Was it still there? Nina did go back and found it had been demolished. I went back while writing my book on Mother to see what remained, and discovered it was now a modern housing development. I spoke with various people in the town, very few of whom knew of the Polish children's home that had been rented by the Polish government-in-exile from the owner, a Sussex lady. When I contacted Nina in Vancouver, where she had settled as a teacher, she remembered all the names of the children who had boarded at Heathfield, although what became of them we never knew. I wonder if they remember it as I do. I met up with Nina's father who was living in London; we had remained friends and reminisced about our time at Heathfield. Nina's father Pan Popowski came from the same area in Belarus—Grodno as my mother. His family name was carved on a remembrance plaque in the Białowieża Forest in Eastern Poland, where Polish men fighting in the resistance were shot. He escaped and hid precious stones in the hem of his coat. He did not reveal his true age to avoid being conscripted into the army. He survived by hiding in the forest with the partisans.

Chapter 4
Poles in Britain

After much reading and research later on in life, I learned of the political struggle the Polish government-in-exile had in their negotiations with their political allies. The Polish military and government-in-exile began to arrive in the UK following the fall of France in 1940.

After Poland had been invaded by Nazi Germany in September 1939, the remainder of the Polish army had joined the French and had fought the Nazis as an 'army in exile'. The unexpected defeat of France led the Polish leadership under General Władysław Sikorski to turn to Britain for help. I remember Mother talking of France and the government-in-exile, but it made little sense to me in those early years.

It is helpful to provide some background as to how so many Poles ended up in Britain, including my mother and the man who was, many years later, to become my stepfather. In July 1941 General Władysław Sikorski, after negotiations between Britain, the Soviet Union and the Polish government-in-exile, signed an agreement that enabled Polish armed forces and civilians imprisoned in the Soviet Union to be freed in order to help fight Hitler. Under General Anders, this mixed group—known as 'Anders' Army'—made their way towards Iran, which was a base for Allied forces.

Mother told me this was how she got out of Russia: via Iran (where she was issued with a Polish passport in Tehran, having lost all her original identity papers) and then on to East Africa as part of the Polish evacuation scheme established by Anders. The priority agreed between the British government and the Polish government-in-exile was to get the Polish refugees back to good health to overcome years of undernourishment and disease. Several camps were set up in British Africa for the Poles, where, among other facilities, children were taught in Polish schools. From here, Poles were offered various countries to settle in, and by March 1944—Mother was in England, serving in Wilmslow, Cheshire, with the Polish forces under British command. That journey from Russia was another ordeal for her.

After the war many Poles settled in London, or close to where their military bases were in Manchester, Scotland and other parts of the UK.

Those Poles who came over as part of Anders' Army's, evacuation scheme settled mainly in London. There, they would have connections with the various Polish émigré associations, cultural clubs, voluntary and government organisations. Emphasis was placed on education in the Polish language and culture, and on maintaining a 'Polishness' quite distinct from that of Soviet Poland.

The community was keen for Mother to maintain her Polish cultural connection, whilst being aware that there must be some aspects of the war she, like many of them, would want to forget. Voluntary and social organisations were important elements of Polish culture and the émigré population was always spontaneously getting together, uniting people in common causes. Mother's life in London was a mixture of engaging with the Polish community and maintaining relationships with British friends who were willing to help her. Although I was totally unaware of the political climate at that time, I remember Mother saying to me once, 'When in Rome, we do as the Romans do.' I took this to mean that maybe once her life had been different, but now we had to fit in with other customs. Whenever I questioned her on her pre-war life, however, Mother found it difficult to answer and looked as if she could not find the words.

I remember as a young child seeing a sign in a shop window saying 'No vacancies, Poles, Irish or Dogs'. At the time I did not see the significance, although I was perplexed and wondered why, I asked my mother, but she just shrugged her shoulders and, after hesitating, said that was the way it was. I was very perplexed. The word 'discrimination' had not yet come into my vocabulary. Did the general public really know or understand the impact the Second World War had on Poland, and on those Poles who would be going back to live under a different regime from the one they had left prior to the war? They had fought for a free Poland; they did not want to go back to a tyrannical one under Soviet rule. Poland the site of two catastrophes, one being the Nazi war of conquest against the Polish nation and the widespread murder and eventual enslavement of the Poles and the other was the campaign extermination directed against all Jewish people in Europe and executed mostly on Polish soil. Then came the tyrannical soviet regime.

When I was looking through the archives in Durham when trying to research Mother's movements, I came across newspaper articles articulating concern about mining jobs being lost. The general xenophobia of the time dominated the news, with concern over what was to happen to the Poles who could not be repatriated to their homeland due to the new territorial divisions in their country, carved up as it had been by the politicians of Germany, Russia and Britain. In my adult life, some of my Polish friends have made comments about the betrayal by the British in dividing up Poland, together with Stalin and Roosevelt. I thought Churchill would never have betrayed us though.

Mother once informed me that she had written to Winston Churchill and to Her Majesty the Queen asking for permission to stay in the United Kingdom. I asked for a copy of this letter from the British Archives Library; however, the gentleman dealing with Churchill's letters was not available on the day I was there, and I never did find out if Mother's letter was kept. I do believe Mother wrote it though.

Chapter 5
South London

Mother married Władysław Slowikowski (Tatus) in 1956. Tatus was not someone I initially took to at first. He was stern-looking, a science teacher Mother had met in London while Janusz and I were at Heathfield. She brought him to Heathfield on a couple of occasions. Then one weekend we were informed that he was going to be our father. Mother took Janusz and me to a teashop in the high street in Heathfield, and there was talk of what our fate would be. I was not happy and cried softly that evening into my pillow without anyone knowing. I did not want to share my mother with anyone else. But I did not want to appear ungrateful and went along with it, as everyone seemed pleased for us.

I had always felt 'Uncle Igor', as I called him, was the closest to what a father-figure *should* be. He was a lawyer who looked after Mother and was always there for her and I would have liked him to have stood in as my father. He was much older than Mother, and he called her his 'little one'. I later found out Uncle Igor's real name was Ignatio Lachowicz, and he acted as a witness to Mother's marriage. At the end of the nineteen fifties he returned to Poland, having traced his own wife and family. In hindsight, I wish I had tried to stay in touch with him; however, getting on with my own life seemed more important at the time. It was only as I began to write this story that I realised how large a role he played in our lives during that time, and how much he must have known about my family's past. His knowledge would have been invaluable for my research.

The house we lived in after Janusz and I left Heathfield and Mother now married was an Edwardian terrace, Number 28, Ennersdale Road, Hither Green in South London; a place of dark, grey streets, terraced houses and a corner shop selling vegetables, a newsagent's, a grocer's and an off-licence at the end of the road. Tatus rented the flat and in turn sub-let one of the rooms to a Mr Bradford.

We lived on the second floor. The flat was clean and I shared a bedroom with Janusz. It all seemed very pre-war, with wood so polished you could almost see your face in the shine. Mother was an avid cleaner especially at Easter time, when the furniture was specially polished even though it already looked clean to Janusz and me. Easter eggs were painted in the traditional Polish fashion and special food bought from a Polish delicatessen in Lewisham. An all-sugar lamb was always an Easter treat.

Living in Hither Green was quite different to the countryside of Heathfield. I had violin lessons, however, practising was not a pastime I enjoyed. It was pointed out to me later that the ability to play a musical instrument had saved many prisoners interned in the German camps. I don't remember having many toys. We made our own entertainment by raiding pots and pans from the kitchen and pretending we were in the Wild West, our open cupboard representing a wagon train, inspired by a favourite television programme of the time. On one occasion Mother held a party in the tiny flat, with Polish friends dancing to the radio, Tango foxtrots and waltzes, they were all good dancers. Mother particularly liked the music of Paul Robeson and Mario Lanza. Two friends in particular who lived close by were childhood friends of Tatus. Lewisham, close to Hither Green, had a Catholic church where Mass was conducted in Polish at certain times on a Sunday, also a Polish delicatessen. Where a barrel of Polish cucumber seasoned with dill sat outside the shop. The beginning of a Polish community—a church, and a shop.

There was a particular gentleman who would come for tea at Ennersdale Road. I say it was tea, however, fuelled with alcohol. As ever, we were not allowed to talk about the war, and just made general conversation. He seemed odd, rather unkempt; a friend of my stepfather's from his war days in Monte Casino maybe, or a fellow Pole in the community. One day he never came back. I was told that he had killed himself. "Why?" was my immediate response.

"Sometimes these things happen when life is too much," Mother replied. I sensed she wanted to expand on this but she stopped herself. "That is the way it is," she said. I think he drank too much. There was always a ready supply of Tatus's home-made wine. He prided himself at his ability to make wine out of almost anything including potatoes. As was his ability to pick mushrooms from the woods and create wonderful dishes from the mushrooms picked, always cooked in butter. Alcohol was one way to deal with the trauma post-war. Many of the prisoners who survived the camps experienced survivors' guilt, as has been recorded in the number of memoirs written by camp survivors. Trauma can be suffered in excess of what the psyche can absorb.

I know Mother would have liked to own a house; however, it was impossible to buy a house. Stepfather's salary as a supply teacher was not enough to meet the repayments; his Master's degree in Botany from the Jagiellonian University in Kraków was not a recognised teaching qualification in Britain, although he was later accepted to teach Science and Biology in the East End of London. When marking the school children's homework, he had meticulous handwriting and made corrections in red pen. War had interrupted his university days when he was conscripted into the Polish Army. He served with the Polish 11 corps stationed at Monte Casino under General Anders, where many Polish soldiers met their death. He would talk about his time in the army and when telling us about 'The Red Poppies on Monte Casino', a patriotic Polish song, his eyes would fill with tears. Many Poles died in this battle. On arriving in the UK, he was stationed in Scotland under General Maczek, where he taught English to the Polish troops who came over with Anders' Army from Siberia. Many of the troops spoke little English and Tatus having a university education where English had been taught was proficient enough for this task.

My stepfather had two sisters, Janka and Stefa, who were also teachers, while his brother worked in a bank. All three remained in Poland during the war. Their father was the Station Master at Nowy Sącz and lived in a lovely little house in Sunshine Street. I visited the house many years later and found Janka still living there in her eighties, chopping wood and with no television. She has since sadly passed away. I felt a sense of happy times in Nowy Sącz before the war.

In the early years of their marriage, my mother and stepfather would send parcels to Poland containing medicines and Max Factor makeup for Janka and Stefa. His brother and one sister came over to the UK in the mid-sixties for a visit. I took them to the Biba shop in Kensington run by Barbara Hulanicki, mainly to show how Polish people settling here had managed to create a good life for themselves. They went home with many gifts, especially medicines, which at that time were difficult to obtain in Poland under Soviet rule.

Once my brother Mark and then Diana came along, in 1958 and 1961 respectively, my parents had to ask the tenant living in one of the rooms to leave so that we could have his room as a bedroom. His room was very messy and he did not venture out much, but I felt sad that he had to give it up and hoped he would find alternative accommodation. Sub-letting the flat was one way to supplement Tatus's salary as a supply teacher.

Although I had no idea at such a young age that I would ever contemplate writing this story, every experience was laid down in my memory. I knew I had an interesting and varied family past, but I don't think I even wanted to know what Mother had gone through, knowing how silent she was at times and how distressed it made her feel. I had learned it was better to just be obedient. Of course, my curiosity in later life got the better of me.

Chapter 6
Siblings

In the two years before my siblings were born, Janusz, Mother, my stepfather and I settled down to a family life similar to the other families around me. We would go away on holiday to Brighton and Eastbourne, staying in a Polish guest house with other Polish nationals. I remember feeling more in tune with my surroundings and loved being with Polish guests. We spoke both Polish and English, or rather Janusz and I spoke in English and Mother replied in Polish. There was no talk of life 'back home' in Poland and as more English was being spoken at home, I got a sense of everyone becoming more British.

I remember in 1957 Mother receiving Christmas parcels from the Red Cross containing items such as toothpaste and toothbrushes, although we already had these things. As to when the parcels stopped and why, I don't know.

Mark was the first child to be born at Ennersdale Road, in 1958, and there was great excitement in buying a pram and other things that went with a new baby. Mother did not work after her marriage and my stepfather's work as a supply teacher brought in very little money. Father tended his garden, which was on one side of the house; the couple who lived downstairs had the other side and it was very neglected. We felt a sense of pride in our side of the garden. My stepfather, having studied Botany at university and later teaching Biology, was never happier than when digging in the garden and buying plants.

Our neighbours, Mr and Mrs Hollis, who lived next door, were a lovely English couple. Their house was divided into two, with their daughter and her husband living on the upper level. They were good to me and gave me a book entitled *Daddy Long Legs*—they would often see me reading and then having being called in to do some chores. They liked to play tricks, like baking what looked like a lovely pie, only to reveal it was full of soil. Janusz and I thought this was all very jolly. Our neighbours were kind, and liked Mother.

I went to the local primary school that is still there today. We also went to summer camp in the holidays, where I remember a lot of dancing out in the rain, which was rather wonderful. I got a prize for 'best bed maker', due to my hospital corners. At home, Janusz and I were allowed to play in the Territorial Army barracks just behind the property and beyond the railway line in Ennersdale road. One of the young boys' father was caretaker. We would play on the stage and hide under the silk parachutes that were left lying around. We would meet up with some of the other children from the neighbourhood. Mother did not mind us playing out as she was busy with looking after Mark and knew we were not far away. We would often play out on the street or buy sweets from the local newsagent.

My sister Diana arrived in 1961, three years after Mark, and was followed in 1963 by Barbara, by which time we had moved from Ennersdale Road to Watermead Road in Catford. We were given a pre-war council house so that we could have a bedroom each. Again the garden was neatly kept by Tatus. There is an age difference of twelve years between Mark and myself. It was strange to learn that neither Diana nor Barbara ever knew I was their half-sister and Janusz their half-brother. They automatically thought that we were all biologically connected. My siblings were told much later on after I had left home. There appeared little need for mother to explain to my siblings anything of her previous life. After the younger children were born, life began to change. Mother suffered a miscarriage before Diana was born and subsequently suffered bouts of depression, alongside addiction to amphetamines and later on alcohol…

Coming home from school one day, I was excited because a friend was coming home with me to enjoy tea. A quiet had descended on the terraced house in Ennersdale Road. There was the smell of smoke rather than the usual smell of freshly washed stairs of red linoleum. We walked up to the flat to find my quiet but distraught mother. "There has been a fire in the downstairs meter cupboard. I am all right, but it might be best if your friend goes home," she said. My disappointment—although familiar—was crushing. No one was hurt, but I wondered how such a thing could happen; I wondered again when fire broke out in our next house in Watermead Road, when my siblings were hurt and ended up in hospital, as did both parents. Again, it was a faulty meter that had set light to the upstairs where everyone was sleeping. All managed to escape but my family were left with scarred memories.

Many of Mother's papers, including photographs and letters, were destroyed in the fire, although some were saved. It always amazes me how many photographs were taken of Janusz and me as babies and when we were growing up. There are numerous pictures taken by professional photographers: no dates, just the photographs, carefully placed in albums. If the photos had not been rescued then this book would never have been written. As it was, the letters that I recall, in their distinctive Par Avion envelopes, were all destroyed. What a wealth of information that would probably have supplied! It makes me think of countries being destroyed by fire and bombs, and how the thoughts, feelings and experiences of those who experience such destruction vanish with them. Mother survived the physical encounters of war but whether she did so psychologically is another matter.

Among the papers and photos that did survive, I found a Post Office savings book in my name, dated 1947, the year I was born, with annual deposits of two shillings and six pence in the four years we were living in Durham. The Post Office told me I could redeem the money, but when I sent the book off I heard nothing more for quite some time. Then, out of the blue, a letter came with a cheque for the amount plus interest added, this amounted to about £20, plus a few pence together with an apology for the long delay. The post box had been set alight but fortunately the savings book was only partially burnt, and it was traced back to me. Fire does seem to have played a frequent role in Mother's story.

I don't want to dwell too much on our life at Ennersdale Road as it is not the reason for writing Mother's story, but some elements are pertinent, for example the arrival of a certain gentleman called Dr Slowikowski, who shared a surname with my stepfather. According to Mother, after the war he was, like so many people, tracing lost family. She told me he was a very important gentleman and was living in Switzerland and London. We went on a family outing with him to Beckenham Park, where Janusz and I danced around, climbing trees, and I remember him saying how happy we looked. I wish now that I had been privy to their conversations.

Dziennik Polski, the Polish daily paper, was widely read by post-war Poles in the UK with notices of people searching for lost family members. 'Uncle Igor' had found his wife was still alive in Poland in the late 1950s and returned home to Poland. Prior to her second marriage Mother did seek to meet a Polish person. She met a Polish gentleman in Brighton; when I asked how it went, she replied that he had five children already, so that seemed to lead nowhere. I expect it was our security she was concerned about. Of course, she would have been very lonely at times and it is no surprise that she wanted to find a husband.

Mother never searched for any of her relatives as she had wistfully told me they had all perished having been shot. Who, when and how I now wanted to know. It was that sad look that stopped me from asking more questions. The reality of the Holocaust was further brought home to me when Mother asked a Polish Jewish lady she was friendly with in Lewisham to show me the distinctive black numbers tattooed on her forearm. It was difficult to know what to say or how to respond; this visual evidence transcended all words and provided me with a living link to the horrors of the war, together with a greater realisation of what Mother and her family had gone through.

Many of Mother's friends in the UK were women who would be working at home machining various garments such as babies' plastic pants. The women would work as they spoke; they had to produce so many garments for a fixed wage. I was encouraged never to ask questions that would upset any of them, so I mainly remained silent and just observed. Were these women friends she had known in the camps?

From the little I knew of the war that my mother experienced, I had a muddled sense that Poles and Jews were the same as so many had been sent to the concentration camps. Even though I was told my mother was not Jewish it was not until much later on, when I began to read the history of the Holocaust, that I realised the difference. There is no way of knowing whether any of her distant family were Jewish, Russian Orthodox or any other faith. Maybe the crucifix she wore with the four crosses made her feel safe. It is poignant to recall that although she went to mass on Sunday she never went to Holy Communion.

Chapter 7
Discovering Durham

Once I had left home, married and borne two children, my mind was distanced from Mother, except when there was some crisis or other. But in the early 1970s, when I decided to visit Durham, where Mother had first lived after her discharge from the Women's Auxiliary service after the war, and where she worked as a nurse at the Durham hospital. My only recollections of her nursing experience are the hospital corners she taught us in making our beds, and a nursing belt she kept; she also sometimes talked about her life working in the hospital and of some of the patients.

I visited the family she stayed with, in Durham and they asked me who the important-looking gentleman was who would come to see her. I remembered him, but at that time was not sure of the relationship. I was later told by my stepfather that he was her lawyer and his name was Ignatio Lachowicz. It was he who Mother contacted when she wanted to leave Durham. I did ask her later on why we left Durham. She replied London was a better place for me to go to school. My first memory of Mother is of us holding hands and walking through the streets of Durham with large bill boards surrounding the area and lots of steep streets. I remember the bedroom we slept in, the chickens in the yard. Revisiting it so many years later, I was surprised how small it was and understood why she had wanted to leave Durham. I can't remember the name of the lady who took Mother into her home, just her kind face and broad Durham accent. She was delighted when she got my letter years later asking to visit the house I remembered as a child, although by this time she and her daughter had moved away from that little terraced house to a modern estate on the outskirts of the city. Her only regret that her husband was not able to see me having died a few years earlier. I understood that Mother had left Durham abruptly and had not left a forwarding address. Naturally they were concerned for my welfare at the time of her leaving.

Little information was gleamed from my visit as to who my father was or where I was conceived. As I was told he was a doctor, could he have been working in the same Durham Hospital, all I know at the time of my visit was what Mother had told me. Her first marriage in Russia had been to Mikolai Karczewski, as was stated on her refugee personal records and it is easy to speculate whether this was the same person who came over to work in Durham. It was when her refugee documents were released to me, I noticed she had described her husband as being deceased.

My Durham visit led me to abandon any idea of further research or questions as, while it had answered some questions, it had left many others unanswered. It was fifteen years before I returned to my search for answers about the past. A visit to Poland with my childhood friend Nina in 2007 prompted that decision, when we visited the Polish War Records Office in Warsaw and the Army Office outside the capital. At the time I had too little information for them to start with except the name of my mother and grandparents together with their dates of birth. Although the authorities tried to be helpful, they were unable to tell me anything about my grandfather. I had Mother's old address in Marszałkowska Street, but could find no record of whether her father had owned or rented the property. I had no record of where her father had been born except to know he came from Warsaw and at some point lived as an Army Officer in Grodno. I did receive a photo from the Community Records Office of what the house in Marszałkowska Street had looked like in 1939, but when I visited the street I could not find No. 31; there was a bombed-out section between the end of the property and the church next door. Mother did once say that there was a church close to where she had lived. The church I saw survived the war intact.

My guide while I was visiting Poland helped me realise how difficult it had been for the Polish people, being invaded by both the Germans from the west and the Russians from the east: it was hard to tell which the worse enemy was. Long before the Russian war crimes at Katyn were acknowledged Mother would speak of their mass execution of Polish people; she, too, hated both the Germans and the Russians, probably in equal measure. It was only when talking about the war in a generalised way or talking about politics that she was more animated and expressed a view. I understood her to be a liberal and egalitarian at heart and would not impose her views on anyone. Her love of Adam Mickiewicz, Poland's national poet was unquestionable. At the time of Mickiewicz's writing in 1795 Poland had ceased to exist as a sovereign state. In 1918 the independence of Poland was proclaimed. As a young person she would have been familiar with his writing and poetry. Now she had witnessed once again Poland no longer free and under foreign control. Mother like most poles would have been brought up to believe that the liberation of Poland would never cease to exist, as proved true after the Solidarnosc Movement in the 1980s. It is sad to know that she never lived long enough to witness this.

Chapter 8

Mother's War and Medical Records

I was disappointed not to discover any records of my mother's family from the Polish archives; I was told this was mainly a result of the chaos the war had brought. I knew that Mother had arrived in Great Britain with General Anders' evacuation scheme, which led me to investigate whether she had any further connection with the military. I was indeed given access to Mother's war records from the Ministry of Defence and the Army Records Centre (Polish) in the UK.

The Refugee personal records held on her arrival in the UK when she was interviewed, giving her personal details, date of birth, parents' names and her address in Warsaw. In the interview she describes herself as a widow, her spouse as Mikolaj Karczewski (deceased). Her address in Warsaw is listed as 31 Marszalkowska, Leszno 1 district. Her occupation she states as Nursing Sister. Her religion as Roman Catholic. What I know from Mother's army records, which had been verified by a Polish medical officer, is that she did in fact enter Russia on 13 April 1940 to the North District of Siberia and was imprisoned there. I also know that she had escaped from the prisoner-of-war camp at Belsen in Germany 1939—and was shot in her left shoulder. She escaped to the Ukraine and it was from there she was recaptured and sent to the Gulag. Following the negotiations between the Polish government-in-exile, Britain and the Soviet Union, it was agreed to allow the release of Polish military and civilians from Russian POW camps, she came from Siberia with the Polish army across the Caspian Sea to Iran, from there to India and with the transport of Polish civilian people to Tanganyika (now

Tanzania) in East Africa, and there to the Polish settlement camp at Kidugala.

The report says she had been a nurse on the ship going with the Polish transport from Karachi (then still part of India, now Pakistan) to Dar es Salaam in Tanganyika. She was stationed at the Polish settlement in Kidugala up to the end of 1943. During that time, her records state she made two attempts on her life.

In conversations I overheard, Mother talked about being made to lie on the floor with rats crawling over her body and being told to jump into the cold sea to see how they would survive while she was in Russia. I did not ask her to expand on these events, it was enough to know that she had suffered and how cruel that time of her capture had been. In *The Eagle Unbowed*, Halik Kochanski writes: 'Life in exile was a psychological struggle as much as a physical one. There are no statistics for the level of mental breakdown amongst the exiles, and while suicides were not unknown, little reference is made to them.' Mother's own wish to die did not subside, but continued after the war, as her medical notes that I was later given access to reveal.

Mother kept the army sewing kit she was issued with during this period, showing the date and place as 1944, Freetown in Sierra Leone, West Africa, with her name in her own distinctive handwriting on the inside flap. I have photographed it as evidence of Mother's time there. It is strange to think that the sewing kit was an everyday item for us growing up, yet only now does its significance hit home. I have two photographs showing Mother in Camp Ifunda, Tanganyika, dated 10 December 1942; there is also one labelled 'Wacław Karczewski, 9 October 1944, the Polish School at Camp Koya in Uganda' in memory. The Polish passport she was issued in Tehran was noted as being dated 18 July 1942. This would indicate that for two years she was based in South Africa at Camp Ifunda.

Mother was conscripted into the Auxiliary Air Force under British Command on 13.3.1944 and transferred to the Polish Women's Auxiliary Air Force on 19 March 1945 until finally discharged. Mother's actual date of arrival in the UK is not known. I have two photographs of her stationed in Wilmslow in Cheshire on 27 June 1944. She worked in the photographic division developing film taken by the pilots and others on reconnaissance. She was honourably discharged in June 1946. After the war she worked briefly for Ilford, developing pictures. I have one she developed of my wedding day, blown up in black and white. Mother was very proud when presenting me with this picture.

I was able to access Mother's medical records after contacting my own GP about my research; he managed to obtain them on my behalf. The accompanying letter said that the records should only be given to the bearer if it was seen that she was of sound body and mind. The records show that she was hospitalised on numerous occasions, as a result of a nervous breakdown and general ill health. They labelled her as histrionic, manic depressive and suicidal. How could anyone come through the German and Russian camps, surviving what she had been through, and not in some way experience psychological anguish? One particular letter I later discovered in her possession was from one of the nursing nuns in the hospital, a moving note that Mother kept until her death.

After reading these documents a lot started to make sense to me, although there were still many unanswered questions. I was working as a psychologist in clinical practice at the time, and so had colleagues I was able to talk to about Mother's medical notes. One psychiatrist in the team recognised the military psychiatric emblem on the medical notes. Psychiatric records are, apparently, the only records kept by the military.

I visited the Sacred Heart maternity home in Milnthorpe, just outside Kendal, where I was born in 1947, and was told that I was lucky Mother had been allowed to take me home, as most mothers there at this time were unmarried and were not permitted to keep their children. Was her assertion that she was married and her husband was abroad enough to convince the nuns to let her keep me? Mother was very persuasive. Perhaps her having worked in a hospital, living in a family home and apparently with a husband somewhere in South Africa would have helped influence the nursing sisters.

As seemed to be the general case in my research, I was informed that no documentation from Mother's time there existed. Maintaining records had not been a legal requirement before 1946, when the NHS Act came into effect, so the home held no medical records in 1947.

I was flagging in my efforts to find out more about Mother's past and gave up for a while, but in 2010 an eminent British historian, Professor Norman Davies, an expert in Polish history who came to stay when I opened my house to the Borders Book Festival in 2010, encouraged me to continue with my research. His first wife had been Polish and he came with his second wife, also Polish. I talked to him about my discoveries and showed him the information that I had gathered to date. I had many questions to ask and with the evidence given by the Home Office and the Russian authorities with evidence of her birth and details of her parents. A picture began to emerge. He enlightened me as to how Polish wartime history of General Anders and various treaties, fitted in with what little Mother had told me. Professor Davies has published a book on General Anders' Army, *Trail of Hope*, and it was he who put me on the right track regarding the deportations to the gulag and the subsequent release into Anders' Army to serve under British command. I had previously not made the connection between General Anders and the release of prisoners in the Soviet Gulag or even questioned what the polish people were doing in the Gulag. Many people even today are not aware of the mass deportations of the Poles to the German concentration camps and to the Soviet camps in Siberia. I thought Russia was fighting with the British against the Germans. Yet Stalin had another agenda as the crimes of Katyn were later revealed. I now understood the reason for Mother being in South Africa.

While we consider the march of the Nazis into Poland in 1939, the Soviet Union had in its sights the total overthrow of the previous Polish political system together with the social, economic and cultural structures. Polish laws were no longer valid and all Polish institutions were disbanded and replaced. Landowners were stripped of their property in preparation for the compulsive collectivisation. Schools and universities, and all churches and synagogues were closed. Russian was introduced as the principal language and all the inhabitants, irrespective of their wishes, were registered soviet citizens. Anyone who dared to object was promptly arrested and sent to the camps. Mother's father was a Captain in the Polish Army, one of the professionals sent to the Gulag camps and or shot. The Polish government have not been able to discover their whereabouts. Mother never knew where her father ended his fate. I think it was easier for her to say he had been shot.

Knowing something about Mother's past yet somehow not connecting it to the actual reality of what happened to her during the Second World War, made me more determined than ever to piece together her story. I had not been aware of the camps set up in Russia before and after the Second World War. I have been unable to find the actual camp Mother was sent in Russia except to know it was in the North district. I now had to systematically go through what I had researched and match it up with what Mother had told me, to somehow piece the jigsaw together and make sense of it all. I was determined to link up the information I had gathered so far. My own recollections of living with Mother during those early days just after the war proved vital in helping me remember and understand how she must have coped, as she was unable to put her experiences into words.

My earlier readings before embarking on this project included *One Day in the Life of Ivan Denisovich*, *Cancer Ward* and *The Gulag Archipelago* by Aleksandr Solzhenitsyn, *The Silver Sword* by Ian Serraillier and *Exodus* by Leon Uris. Mother herself was interested in Boris Pasternak, and she read *Doctor Zhivago* (published in 1957). Her own interest was in the Russian Revolution and the battle between the White Russians and the Red Army. Her greatest love was of the Polish author Adam Mickiewicz, particularly his collected poetry and the epic *Pan Tadeusz*. Mother would argue about political events of the day. It was obvious that she did not accept the Russian position in Poland and was adamant that she would not return. In fact she could not return for fear of reprisals due to her record of escape. I deeply regret that she did not live to see a free Poland. Since undertaking this research my reading has extended to vast historical, autobiographical and archive data on the Second World War. I am now what one would term 'a historical junkie.' Had Mother been alive today this would have been an inroad to her particular story and probably would have made her less fearful of being judged.

Chapter 9
Belarus

Having decided to continue with my research, I took a journey to Belarus via Poland with my second husband. As we approached the Belarus border an army officer asked us for our passports. Mine, however, was not returned. I became very worried and when I showed signs of distress a young woman came up to me and told me not to worry, it had happened to her also on her last visit. Her name was Barbara and she lived just over the border in Białystok, Poland, where we had travelled from. Barbara travelled frequently to visit her fiancé, who lived in Grodno. This couple became our friends and helped us navigate our way around Grodno.

We paid a visit to the Oblast State Archive Scientific Authority, to give it its correct title. I paid a fee, but it was several years later that I received official documents in the name of 'Stefan Gwizdalski, born 1898, the son of Anton and Anna, lived with his wife Maria Gwizdal'skaya, born 1899, and daughter Lyutsiya (name as shown on document), born 1922, Grodno at 11 Ulitsa Grandichskaya. The house was registered in 1885'. No other information has been found in the archives on the Gwizdalski family. It is signed by Deputy Archive Director. I did ask if there were any photographs and was told, "No photographs". Did this mean there were none, or, 'We are not letting you have any'?

It was Barbara and her now-husband Walery (pronounced Valery) who later hunted for the address. It is now known as Gorki Street. However, the numbers had not changed. It was a grand street according to Walery and Barbara. Walery has since sent me a picture of how a new house built looked today their old house having been demolished. Walery very kindly asked among the older generation whether anyone remembered the family who lived there, but drew a blank.

In 1922 Grodno was part of the Polish province of Białystok. Records I had previously obtained from the Polish Army Records Centre, then in Hayes, Middlesex, also named Mother's parents as Stefan and Maria Gwizdalski, née Kaziulonis. At the time of Mother's birth in 1922, her father would be age 24 and her mother age 23. The Russian revolution of 1917 and the First World War 1914–1918 nearing its completion. Poland prior to 1900 had been surrounded by Russia, Prussia and Austria-Hungary. It gained its independence in 1918 under Joseph Pilsudski. Poland had experienced a troubled past.

As I walked through the streets of Grodno, I had a sense of Mother's history and wondered whether her parents had walked these same streets, pushing her in her pram. How close it made me feel towards them. The old town of Grodno is very beautiful; many of the streets remain cobbled, lined with beautiful old buildings, if a little unkempt. Of course, there were also Soviet-style flats in their grey, uniform high-rise blocks. People on the whole seemed contented under the controlled regime still under Alexander Lukashenko, President since 1994.

On a visit to a Polish exhibition in one of the castles high up on a hilltop I got a sense of how Polish people lived during those years in 1922. It was a good life for the Poles here, I was told by the curator. It certainly took me back to *Pan Twardowski* the book from my childhood and *Pan Tadeusz* written by the poet Adam Mickiewicz, whom Mother had often spoken about. Janusz has her book of his poems. He was born in Vilnius, Lithuania, which is where her mother Maria was also born. Maybe this is as close as I am going to get to my grandparents and mother's early life. The past appears to be a blank canvas on which I must paint whatever scene I choose to imagine as to what my grandparents were like, what kind of life did they led, whether they were rich or poor, country or city folk. What of their education; their hair colour and height? Did they like music, could they paint and dance? I can hope that one day the future generations of my family might find it in their hearts and minds to further search for their ancestors. The opening up of documents and archive research might reveal more of their identities.

My journey back to Białystok was one reminiscent of the Stalin era with contraband being smuggled, passports confiscated and questioning as to my reason for being in Belarus. I do want to go back to Belarus some day. The need to travel to Vilnius and search for information about my grandmother feels more of a priority and reveals a further piece of the jigsaw.

Chapter 10
Questions

History has documented that when the Germans invaded Warsaw in 1939, Polish officers were either shot or sent to the camps. In fact, groups of ordinary Polish people were rounded up and sent to the camps (as recounted in Norman Davies' *God's Playground*). However, as an army officer, Mother's father, Stefan Gwizdalski, would have served under the Russian army in Belarus and/or the post-revolutionary Socialist regime, and was therefore an enemy of Germany. He might have tried to escape imprisonment, but whatever happened, the outcome was that he was shot. Military hospital records reveal that Mother's father was a doctor in the Polish Consular Service and an army officer. Mother was the youngest in a family of five, and I understand that her four older brothers were also killed. She had stated on arriving in the UK that she was an only child. There are conflicting statements to her replies to the British authorities in relation to her family in Poland. The records state she met her husband in Russia, was married and had a child who died of Typhus. She herself also suffered from Typhus. She was liberated with the Polish Army to Persia, from Persia to India and then to East Africa. She finally came to England in March 1944 when she joined the Polish Women Auxiliary Air Force under British command. This fits in with what she had told me over the years. She told me that her mother died in 1939. A distant look veiled her face whenever anyone asked her about her family, which inhibited our questioning, but it feels very strange not knowing what my grandparents were like. Where did they actually die and where were they buried? Many a graveyard I have walked looking for a glimpse of the Gwizdalski name or to see a plaque listing them among those who died. I have always wondered about them and have ended up inventing my own image of what my grandparents looked like.

It was when working through her life and attempting to join up all her movements with the information gathered, that I had the brainwave to contact Social Services with regard to the events regarding the fires at our homes, especially the one in Watermead Road. I thought she might have revealed to someone further details about her past, especially when we were adopted by our stepfather and having to go through the courts, and/or her life during the war. She gave no name, of our father although the story of her marriage in Russia appears here. It was also repeated that she had a child in Russia who died of typhus and was named Maria after her own mother. Most startling of all for me was to read that she was in Auschwitz and Belsen concentration camps. She survived Belsen by hiding herself under dead bodies which were to be burnt with lime the following day. Mother saw a way to run away and was then shot in the shoulder, recaptured and sent to Siberia. For me it was the knowledge that it was Belsen concentration camp that disturbed me the most and seeing it written down in black and white. It seems Mother was always running away. Mother had never voiced which camp she was actually in.

Works by Jewish writers like Eva Hoffman (who I met many years later), Tadeusz Borowski and Halik Kochanski graphically and eloquently document the work that went into preparing for the Holocaust, and report the vast numbers of the Polish population, and others, who were forced into the work camps. Not to cooperate would have meant death just as surely as cooperating usually did. "Would you put your head in the Gas oven?" she once asked me when I was quite young.

"No," I replied, not realising the significance of her statement. As a child I absorbed her utterances with some sort of detachment.

I will always find it difficult to contemplate what life was like for Mother in the camps and later on in Russia. I only know from the accounts of others how horrendous it must have been: the lack of food, harsh winters, lost family and friends. To see and hear the destruction and treatment of others.

When I picked up my research again, one of my first questions was: why was Mother sent to a concentration camp in the first place? Many of my British friends were under the impression that that only happened to Jewish people. Mother was not Jewish. Or was she? Mother's story to the British authorities at the outbreak of war, working in the hospital in Warsaw together with many others, sent to work in the German camps. Being a young, woman of 18 would have fitted the category of slave labour. Many Polish people *were* detained and/or shot when the Germans invaded Warsaw in 1939, whether or not they were, like my grandfather, in the army. The so-called intelligentsia were also seen as a threat, not just by the Nazis but by the Russians, as the mass killings at Katyn is evidence. My further research showed that the eradication of Poles was systematic, regardless of whether they were Jewish or not. One has to remember that she was born in Belarus, and therefore had a Soviet identity as well as a Polish passport; both became enemies of Germany.

According to history books Belsen was set up as a camp for 'exchange Jews' selected for possible prisoner swaps by the Nazi authorities and throughout its build took on many functions leading to the extermination of the Jewish population sent there. As the camp grew, so did chaos, disease and death, with devastating speed. Prisoners were moved from one camp to another Belsen was also used as a holding camp for the sick and dying from other camps (Nikolaus Wachsmann 2015).

It is my belief based on what Mother told me and her social work records, Mother was sent to Belsen in 1939/40 as slave labour to help build the camp that housed prisoners of war before it became a death camp for the eradication of the Jewish people. Many young Polish women were forced to have sexual contact with German guards and prisoners. In 1939, Mother was a young woman of 18 and very attractive.

What she was made to do, and why, must lie in the German records.

Mother and my stepfather returned to Poland with my siblings much later on, in the 1970s, to visit his family. I was establishing my own married life at that time, and I did not ask how they felt about their visit, but Mark told me that Mother went to Auschwitz and remembered where she had been in the camp; and how upset she became remembering how so many people had lost their lives. Mother never told me why she was sent to Auschwitz. I have no record of her time there. Mark informed me she knew where she was and walked around the camp on her own in deep contemplation. Prisoners who were deemed fit and healthy were moved between the camps, so perhaps she was moved there. It was after her attempted escape from Belsen, when she hid under a pile of dead bodies overnight waiting to be burned in lime, shot in the left shoulder when she emerged to run away, that she was sent to the Soviet camp. Perhaps her Belarusian/Soviet identity was behind this move, although it does not seem to have saved her from harsh treatment by the Soviets. It was a time she did not want to remember. No passport was ever recovered, even the one issued in Tehran has never been recovered amongst her possessions, but then she would have surrendered the passport to gain access on her visit to Poland. Mother was granted British nationality and was given a new passport.

I sometimes wondered whether Mother thought the war was not really over and that conflict would flare up once again. In her heart and mind there was always emotional conflict. My stepfather remained a pacifist, hating the notion of any kind of war. Mother on the other hand would have been ready to fight.

Chapter 11
Possible 'Secrets'?

I have since wondered whether Mother kept so many secrets from me and my siblings because she was ashamed of what had happened to her during the war or what she had to do to survive, or indeed what she had witnessed. When I was twelve and we were on a visit to Brighton Beach, where we would go at weekends by train from New Cross for the day, she was wearing a bathing costume—I saw marks on the inside thigh of her left leg. A horrific sight: part of the skin had been removed and although it had now healed over it looked as if part of the inside leg was missing. I, of course, asked how it had happened and she brushed it aside and said it was an accident; she had fallen off a cliff looking up at the cliffs behind her. I did not believe her and asked whether it hurt. "Not anymore," she replied. That day I learned to swim in the sea, the salt water keeping me afloat. I was surprised that the scar was not covered up. I also learned that day of the healing powers of salt water.

From reading archive data I now understand that she may have been experimented on in the camps. Serum was injected into the body to see how muscle and bone would react. In the camps attractive women were singled out to service the sexual needs of the soldiers. Mother may have been one of those women. It was something you did not go telling people about. I understand women were also given numbers on the upper arm to indicate their profession in the camps. I never saw such a number on her upper arms, as she often wore sleeveless dresses and I would have noticed. Not long after this while living in Ennersdale Road, I remember seeing a green medical book on the bookshelf. On leafing through the pages I saw a picture of what looked like Mother's leg with large numbers beside it and the words 'Nuremberg Trials'. I cannot be sure whether it was the actual picture of Mother's leg. There were pictures of body parts in jars filled with liquid. I promptly took the book through to Mother showing the leg similar to her leg I had seen in Brighton. When I asked what the book was about, the book was immediately taken from me and I never saw it again. I was surprised, thinking about it later on in my life, that it was so quickly dismissed as a nursing book. I wondered how it got to be in her possession. There were many books on the bookshelf in Ennersdale Road, mainly my stepfather's textbooks on Biology, Botany and Zoology. Most of the books never seemed to be read. I would occasionally glance at them on the bookshelf, what made me take that particular book off the shelf I sometimes wonder. As a young girl probably around the age of six and while still at Virgo Fidelis, Aunty Joan would take Mother, Janusz and me in her Austin car on a journey through the Sussex country side; Mother would be dropped off at what looked like a cottage hospital before collecting her again. Aunty Joan later told me it was a specialist burns unit. My mind thinks of skin drafts and what. would have been possible to make her leg less slightly wounded.

On one visit home, when Mother was not well and possibly a spell in hospital was imminent, I stumbled across a small piece of paper in her unmistakable handwriting, which read: 'Tied to a tree and raped by six solders.' Great sadness came over me—yet more suffering and trauma. I believe we all knew some terrible things had happened to Mother, but seeing it written down made it all the more horrifying. Was this when she escaped into the Ukraine, the partisans were well organised although not all survived. The Russians were entering the war from the East and the Germans from the west. I can still see that piece of paper and those words in her handwriting. I did not pick it up, but left it where it was. We all knew she had been raped during the war from past conversations. I was not on my own and pointed it out to my husband Michael. We did not say much but had an unspoken understanding of the piece of paper with those words written on it. It did not state the nationality of the soldiers, was it German or Russian soldiers? In the same way we never know who shot her father, the Russians or the Germans. She clearly had a need in her later life to put what had happened on paper. It is indelibly marked on my memory, and like the sight of her wounded leg and the story of her attempted escape from Belsen, I will never be able to forget it. I can only put it away in the annals of my brain just as she had to do, and try to move on from it. I can so fully understand and feel why she could not talk about her past to me or members of her family. I can only reflect on my reactions and feelings and understand why she was not believed in her early medical reports. I felt emotional in an existential sort of way. Mother could not fend off depression. Even the recognition of her loss and trauma could not set her free.

Having a family was all Mother wanted. It was important to her to experience the birth of her children. However, that in itself would not take the psychological pain of all she had suffered away. I know she loved all her children, and I remember asking her GP on a visit home in my late twenties, "Why can't anyone help Mother?" She had become addicted to benzo, amphetamines and alcohol.

The doctor replied, "No one can help what your mother has been through." I in particular felt helpless and somewhat guilty in not being able to help Mother in her distress at times. Each of us in our own way built up our defence mechanisms in managing our own reactions. She had Tatus and he remained stoical.

Later in life, I became a psychologist and hopefully helped many people through their difficulties. However, it was too late for Mother—I was probably too close. Mother did inform me that she had told her story to a psychiatrist based in Scotland while she was hospitalised after the war. There was a Polish Medical School established in Edinburgh where polish would have been spoken. "He knows everything about me," she informed me once, as if to instil in me the re-assurance that someone did know. Women today are still not believed when they tell of violence towards them, and the fear of stigma often holds them back from telling their stories. I have read many books on the Second World War that focus especially on survivors' stories, most of which chronicle similar accounts of escape and shootings, tortuous train journeys and harsh treatment in the Russian camps.

It felt like I was being fed information in tiny fragments that Mother could not keep suppressed over the course of her life, possibly the same fragments over and over again.

Chapter 12
African Violets

Who was Mother's first husband?

Mother informed the authorities she had married in Russia. (Mikolaj) Karczewski was the name given on her records. She also told the authorities and me that she had lost her first born child in Russia. The child had died of typhus. It was the death of her child she christened Maria after her own mother that tormented her so much. In the horror of the Siberia, this child was all she could hang on to and now even that had been taken away from her.

Africa was mentioned several times by Mother, once in relation to African violets—there were always some in a pot at home. When I asked her why she liked them so much, she told me they reminded her of someone. Again that wistful tone: Mother had that familiar look, as if although she did not want to remember those days, it was still something she felt deeply about. It was always better not to involve her in any great meaningful discussions about her war years, as she would just switch off. No one wanted to trigger a period of depression. I learned from social work records that she had recorded in her notes that her husband was somehow connected to the Mau Mau and was a gunrunner. This was not something she would have just invented or imagined. Could this be why she was hiding his identity? However, she was concerned that a photograph existed sent to her from Camp Fundi in East Africa on the back was the signature of Waclaw Karczewski 9th October 1944. Her refugee records stated her husband's name was Mikolaj Karczewski was this one and the same person or a brother? It was later hinted to me that she was certainly protecting someone. I always had this impression, as well as the sense that she was still in touch with that person prior to my attending Heathfield. Those distinctive airmail letters always hinted to me of correspondence from Africa and/or Poland, although letters would have been censored during the 1950s, depending which country they came from. There is also a photograph of her with an African banana seller. Mother looks in good health and happy. It must have been a relief to experience life and freedom in Africa compared to the camp life in the gulag.

I had once asked Mother who my biological father was, I was seventeen. Mother said it was a complicated issue and she needed to contact Miss Reynolds, a social worker and known to Mother for some time. I was kindly invited for a meeting with her and Mother. I was unable to attend that day as I had an exam and never managed to arrange a different date. It could be that some unconscious motive on my part did not really want to know, as I knew it would be painful yet again for Mother. However, Miss Reynolds became a family friend and subsequently came to my wedding. It is worth noting that in 1954, borders were closed in the Eastern Bloc amid the arrest of wartime resistance fighters and émigrés by the Soviet secret police. My belief is she feared this most of all, as did the vast majority of the Polish armed forces who remained in Britain. On her refugee personal records administration document Mother gave the name of spouse—Mikolaj Karczewski as being deceased. If in fact my biological father was not dead and he had another family somewhere in Poland prior to the war; the anguish this might cause was not something Mother wanted to be reminded of and of course she would have some explaining to do. Maybe it was best that I did not know.

Violets are a symbol of love and faithfulness. I will never know who she was remembering when I asked her about the bowl of African violets that she always had in the house. All I know is that they were a loyal memorial to someone possibly from her African days. To the last, Mother stayed firm in keeping his identity secret. In her continuing suffering there is the comfort in knowing that she did find love in those horrific days. It is interesting to note that had her first husband not died and she wished to marry again then she would be committing bigamy unless a divorce was recorded. My stepfather had informed me that her first husband was not a good man; I took this to mean he must have abandoned her or not wanting to recognise Janusz and myself, if he indeed was our biological father.

Chapter 13
Psychological Trauma

What has kept me going with this research? It is hard to keep going back and racking my brains for any kind of conversation remembered. Sometimes, especially at night, my mind is unable to switch off, so I read a little more and write my thoughts down as if to empty what is in my head. I read and re-read documents and the testimony of other Polish people on that same horrendous journey from Russia. I can see how with trauma one can stop thinking about what happened by switching off and just moving forwards, refusing to look back. However, there will always be reminders that flip the mind back into the past and resurrect unwanted memories one tries to submerge.

People have asked me, "Did you not ask your mother what happened?" I could see how this was difficult for her and was not something she wanted to be reminded of; that she was especially reluctant to tell someone so close to her. It is often easier to tell a complete stranger your story: you know that those closest to you will not be harmed in the telling. So many people in a similar situation kept their emotions buried, as it was safer that way. I am sure if I had asked Mother when she was in her sixties or seventies I might have got a more joined-up story and she might have opened up more.

***

I met Eva Hoffman, the Jewish writer whose books I had read and admired for her sheer eloquence and knowledge of the Holocaust, at a meeting of psychiatrists and psychotherapists in the Lowry Museum in Salford around 1995 where an exhibition of the Second World War was being shown. Her talk about her parents' experience as Polish Jews sent to the extermination camps and of the general malaise of mental health workers in the field of dealing and managing such traumas brought tears to my eyes, which I tried to hold back. She noticed my empathy as she recalled how professions she had encountered exhibited little empathic understanding of her difficulties in being a second generation survivor of the Holocaust as she saw herself. Psychological counselling in the post-war period was mainly left in the hands of psychiatrists and those who had trained in psychotherapy. Training in Psychological Counselling did not come into effect till the late 1950s with the works of Carl Rogers an American Psychologist pioneering a person-centred approach to listening to peoples dilemmas. There was limited mental health provision in the 1950 and 1960s Eva's eloquence and knowledge of the psychological state of the next generation, who had to live with the aftermath and consequences of parents who had suffered under the Nazi regime transfixed me. We talked briefly afterwards and came to the conclusion that it would continue to affect not only the second, but also the third and subsequent generations. That simply not to talk about or share experiences does not mean they will go away or be forgotten. Mother's own reticence and efforts to forget the past have made me doubt whether I should be writing down her experiences or, more importantly, showing what I have written to others. However, the wider silence on the subject, the lack of interest from others, has meant that in many families, not just my own, the secret past is becoming even more of a secret. The kind of silence prevailing amongst survivors has been reinforced, and it seems important to break the silence in order to allow current generations a better understanding of their history and heritage. The act of immigration itself means a loss of the familiar.

The experiences of my mother and other wartime refugees were so horrible and so strange in a country that had never undergone such horrors, that their stories were often not believed. I know memory can be misleading and we can invent things that are not really true, and I think that is how others saw Mother—that what she told them could not possibly be true. And if they did believe her, what could they do? Most people in Britain had no conception of what it was like to have experienced what Mother had gone through. It was only by talking to other Polish people, mostly older than me, and hearing stories of what their parents had gone through in escaping the war, that I could begin to understand.

When I was studying at Manchester University, I wrote an essay on 'Living Between Two Cultures'. I interviewed Polish people who had escaped the war and settled in Manchester, where there was a thriving Polish community. I remember being told how difficult life was for them in those years before they came to Britain, but no one ever actually revealed exactly what treatment they underwent. I think they could not burden me with their experiences but felt it would suffice for me simply to know that it was hard and they had suffered. It was always so difficult for people to articulate their experiences. It seemed I had to learn everything from memoirs some survivors had managed to write and publish.

"My father jumped off the train, on the journey to the camps," one explained.

"I escaped by hiding diamonds in the hem of my clothes, useful for bribing guards," another said. "We spent days in the woods and wading through rivers."

One lady I asked told me, "Oh we never go there, too horrible for words." When I was first married and living in Maidstone, Kent, I joined the young wives of the Women's Institute. In a voluntary capacity, I visited a local psychiatric hospital where there were Polish soldiers and airmen. Traumatised by the war, they carried their suitcases with them wherever they went in the grounds, looking up to the skies, overcoats on ready to be evacuated. Over afternoon tea with one or two of these gentlemen, I would be told in scrambled words some of what had happened to them, although their tales were always mixed with suspicion of me, because I would be talking Polish to them. They had little idea where they were or what was going to happen to them, except that they were ready to move on with their suitcases as they frequently looked up to the skies, wondering where the next bombs were going to land. It made me feel sad how little I, or anyone, could do to help them. There appears to be no therapy for history; it is something we cannot heal or cure.

Chapter 14
Death

Mother rang me one weekend to say that she was in a nursing home for respite from her mental anguish. She begged me to take her home, but my husband at the time, in consultation with the nursing staff, thought it better for her to remain. I was torn, I hated leaving her there. It was full of people older than herself and she seemed coherent, yet puzzled as to why she was there. The following day, I learned that she had walked out of the home, got on a train, presented herself to a police station and was escorted home by a police officer. She was not going to be pushed around by anyone. My stepfather just held up his hands and shrugged his shoulders. It was difficult for him to deal with her at times. I always admired her for her stance and bravery and her determination to have her own way, and to some extent my stepfather for his continuing to care for her.

I visited Mother the weekend she died. We went to buy her a blue velvet dressing gown, something she wanted. She was in a contemplative mood, and I remember a conversation we had on our way home, when she asked me to have faith, as it is, she said, important to believe in something. I read nothing into this conversation at the time, although it has since made me reflect on her own faiths—her conversion to Roman Catholicism and her desire for her children to be brought up in the catholic faith. I still wonder whether she did have a Jewish connection despite being told she did not. When I look at the face of my son Alexander, I see a polish character reminiscent of Pan Twardowski, a truly polish face, as others have told him also.

When I heard of her death the following Saturday I felt a pain just as if a dagger had pierced my heart. I cried out, "Oh no, no." It was not until after Mother's death that I became aware of a large gulf in my knowledge of her life before I was born, and a sadness at not knowing about my own father. I had some glimpses, but they were like sepia prints, something from the distant past. It was several years later that I decided to start finding out more about her life and began to write to the various agencies and government departments.

I have no knowledge of Mother's life before the war except that she was possibly unhappy and found solace in staying with her grandfather who lived in the mountains. At one point she told me her mother had died when she was young, although she informed the authorities she died in 1939. I believe Mother was cared for by an aunt during her younger years after her own mother died. She once took me to see the film *Heidi*, telling me that it reminded her of her grandfather who lived in the mountains.

I still miss her. When experiencing misfortunes in my life, I remain stoical and think to myself, *Listen Anna, this is nothing to what Mother endured. She was a survivor and so must I be.* I carry this thought with me always.

Chapter 15
Mother's Legacy

As a young child growing up in post-war Britain, I had little comprehension of the background to the war. It was difficult for me to understand the consequences of the Second World War: the Cold War, and the collective revenge that was perpetrated upon ethnic Germans as they were expelled from Polish soil. The destruction by the Soviets of the Polish gentry and the people who had struggled honourably against the Nazi regime, who were imprisoned and sent to Siberia. The heroic stance of the Warsaw uprising. The destruction of a beautiful city and way of life for both Poles and Jewish people and especially the continuing post-war violence against the surviving Jewish population. It is difficult to comprehend the trauma of losing your home, and all those close to you. Even losing your country. The word 'trauma' means 'wound', an emotional shock that creates substantial and lasting damage to the development of the individual.

However, there is nothing in Mother's medical notes that mentions the word. The post-war psychiatric and medical professions made little or no connection between extreme kinds of abuse and subsequent mental pain, nor indeed did they understand the experiences of those who became refugees. I doubt they actually believed Mother's story. I found only one entry in her medical war records that verified that the wounds on her leg were not self-inflicted. It was made by a Polish doctor, who must have known what had happened in the camps. It made me feel Mother was always telling the truth, although it was probably difficult for her, bearing in mind the language barrier and her youth. How do you in fact tell your experiences in the clinical environment of a hospital ward? She had survived; therefore, she could rebuild her life. I believe it was the kindness and understanding of the nuns who cared for and listened to Mother's story that helped her the most in the early days of the aftermath of the Second World War, together with the Polish community and the many friends she made In the UK and especially to the kind people who looked after myself and Janusz.

It is difficult to contemplate how Mother survived after the end of the war. She was honourably discharged from military service into civilian life. Friends like Auntie Joan, her work friend Helen, who was Lady of Honour at her wedding and my godmother (although we lost touch with her after that), and Uncle Igor, together with those kind people who took Mother under their wing and helped her get work in hospitals, convents (Torquay) and Polish nursery schools such as the one in Nightingale Lane in the early fifties, funded by the poles themselves with donations from America and elsewhere. These were places where Janusz and I could also be looked after. Many of the childhood photos that survive carefully placed in albums display our sense of happiness and being cared for. It is a great sadness to me that no photographs remain from Mother's own childhood or that of her parents, grandparents and other members of her family.

It has not been an easy process either discovering or writing her story, and at times as I have already mentioned I have wondered whether Mother would have wanted me to put her life onto paper. I could choose to ignore it, but if I did that then what Mother endured would be unacknowledged. I have a fundamental curiosity about my familial past; an urge to know and touch on the geography of my parents' pre-war lives. I have gleamed information from a wide range of sources, including my own early recollections growing up in post-war Britain, also from documents sent to me by the Foreign Office, including army and medical records; from the East African Refugee administration records and visiting the Soviet authorities in Belarus.

I never knew my grandparents, lost in the terrors of war, so on neither side of my lineage were they able to guide me through my curiosity. I do hope to enlighten my own children as to their grandmother's past and answer my grandchildren's questions as they become curious about their family history as and when appropriate to do so.

On a visit to Warsaw, I was once asked, in Polish, by a gentleman in a lift at the Bristol Hotel, who I was. He could tell from my accent that I was not a native of Warsaw.

"I am half Polish and half English," I said.

"Which half of you is Polish?"

I thought of touching my heart.

"Where your heart is!" he interjected.

I smiled as if to say, of course. We parted.

We are all part of historical circumstances. I am enriched with the knowledge of the Polish culture of my parents, and have come to a reconciliation with the difficult nature of that past.

We can reflect on the past, but we don't have to dwell on it. We must learn from history and keep trying to learn. I took my two children to Poland one summer. We paid a visit to Auschwitz so they had knowledge of what the Nazi regime inflicted on the Jewish people and other nationalities, including their grandparents. Their reaction was quiet contemplation. What they do with that knowledge is for them to decide. For the inheritors of traumatic historical experience in the second generation, the ability to separate the past from the present, to see the past as the past, is a difficult but necessary achievement. For Mother, the past was forever present. If I have one regret in life, it is that I was unable to help her more in eliminating her suffering. My siblings took over that role of caring for her after I left home.

Chapter 16
Living Between Two Cultures

When I was studying psychology at Manchester University and again for my Masters in Psychology, the counselling arena was likened to a building, with each floor representing a different level of consciousness. Therapy can remain on one floor for a long time increasingly moving the furniture around so to speak. Why did this strike a chord in me? One, I felt I was operating on one level. I knew there were other levels; I just did not know how to get up or down. My own consciousness kept me safe on one level. There were inspirations of shifts in consciousness from myself; however, upon reflection, I think we only glimpse at other levels. We know they are there, but the safety of the familiar keeps us grounded on one level. It took me a while to be bold enough to attempt to operate psychologically on different levels. I could see out of the window on my safe level. Despite all her efforts, Mother accommodated into the host community. She learnt the language yet kept up her Polish traditions. She married a fellow Pole. She made sure and accepted her children were part of a British community. I always saw her identity as Polish I am not sure you can give up an identity having lived the best part of twenty two years in a culture different to the one she now found herself in. Assimilation came with the second generation and now the third and fourth generations might have no or little knowledge of their Polish past. Do I keep it from them, or tell it in a sanitised way? There are many books written by survivors however, when you are personally close to what happened to someone in your family, I decided against just a historical account and instead I have told it through my own experience, a more personal and poignant experience. Memory can be misleading and faded over time, it can also become a longing for historical events and facts, however once those who have living memory of the events of the second world war are no longer with us we fall back on the written and collective evidence and stories of those affected by the tragedy. Hence it is important that events are not lost or forgotten over time. It does seem perplexing that we continue to ignore the lessons of the past in order to inform a better future.

In my mind I see my mother as a courageous woman, determined on the one hand and completely broken on the other; yet a woman who attempted to get on and rebuild her life in a foreign country. She was unable to go back to Poland as there was nothing or no one to return to; she also feared reprisals from the Russian regime for her escape and did not want to surrender to a Soviet tyranny. She probably would have been sent to prison. Her only option was to move forward and rebuild her shattered life.

When I look back on that train journey to Heathfield, I think how little I knew then and how much I know now. The train moves on to a different destination. However, even today that journey remains a nightmare for many displaced persons due to war and perpetuation of suffering for future generations. It would seem that despite the knowledge we know of human suffering and the continuing escalation of war torn countries, we do not seem to learn the lessons of the past.

Chapter 17
Chronologies

Pre-war

1922 Ludomira Czeslawa Slowikowska formerly Karczewska nee Gwizdalska born Grodno Bialystok Poland

1939	War broke out in Warsaw. Mother working in Polish hospital in the city. Living at 31 Marszalkowska UL Warsaw, Leszna 1 district. Captured and sent to camp in Belsen and Auschwitz.
1940	Escaped from Belsen—shot in left shoulder while escaping, recaptured and sent to Siberia North District.
1941	Married Mikolaj Waclaw Karczewski, daughter (Maria) born, who died of typhus. Mother suffered from amnesia.
1942, February	Released from Russia to General Anders' Army in the Middle East.
1942, August	Arrived in Iran via Caspian Sea in the second wave of refugees from Russia. Issued with a Polish passport, No. 05281/42. Moved on to East Africa (Tanganyika/Uganda).
1944	Serving in Freetown, West Africa. Issued with sewing kit.
13.03.1944–06.1946	Served with Polish forces under British command WAAF/PWAS. Wilmslow, Cheshire.

13.04.1944	Joined the Polish Women's Auxiliary Air Force under British command at RAF Station Redcar UK in the rank of Aircraftwoman 2, in the trade of Aircraft hand/General Duties—service number 2792465.
08.06.1944	No. 32 Reception Centre RAF Station Wilmslow.
13.07.1944	Polish Air Force Depot Blackpool.
02.08.1944	Admitted to the RAF Hospital at Kirkham.
15.09.1944	Returned to the Polish Air Force Depot, Blackpool.
09.10.1944	Photo of Waclaw Karczewska at Koja Polish School Uganda.
22.11.1944	Admitted to St Andrews Military Hospital for Women, Northampton.
19.03.1945	Discharged from Polish Women's Auxiliary Air Force and transferred to the Polish Women Auxiliary Service (PWAS) posted to I PWAS Company, I Polish Corps—served in Scotland (location not recorded).
15.04.1946	Admitted to No. 11 Polish General Hospital for record purposes—actually treated at English Civilian Hospital Ford, Sussex.
11.06.1946	Declared unfit for auxiliary military service—discharged.
[date]	Awarded British War Medal 1939–45 (CS20).

Post-war

1947 I was born, Mother living and working in Durham at a psychiatric hospital.

1950 Janusz born. Family now living in Birmingham and Torquay. Mother working in St Mary's Convent.

1952 56 Living in Crystal Palace. (Janusz and I at Virgo Fidelis and Heathfield.)

1956 Mother's marriage to Władysław Slowikowski; moved to Hither Green, Catford, South London. 1957 Janusz and I adopted Bromley courts.

1958 Mark born.

1961 Diana born.

1963 Barbara born.

22.04.1979 Mother died. Age 55. Service held in Brockley, South London. Buried in Hither Green Cemetery.

Anna Karczewska Slowikowska

Ludomira Gwizdalska – RAF Wilsmslow, Cheshire, 1944

Mother Janusz and I at my first Holy Communion – Virgo Fidelis, London

Mother, first row, far right end of the row

Ludomira Gwizdalska, 1950

Marriage to Wladyslaw Slowikowski, 1957

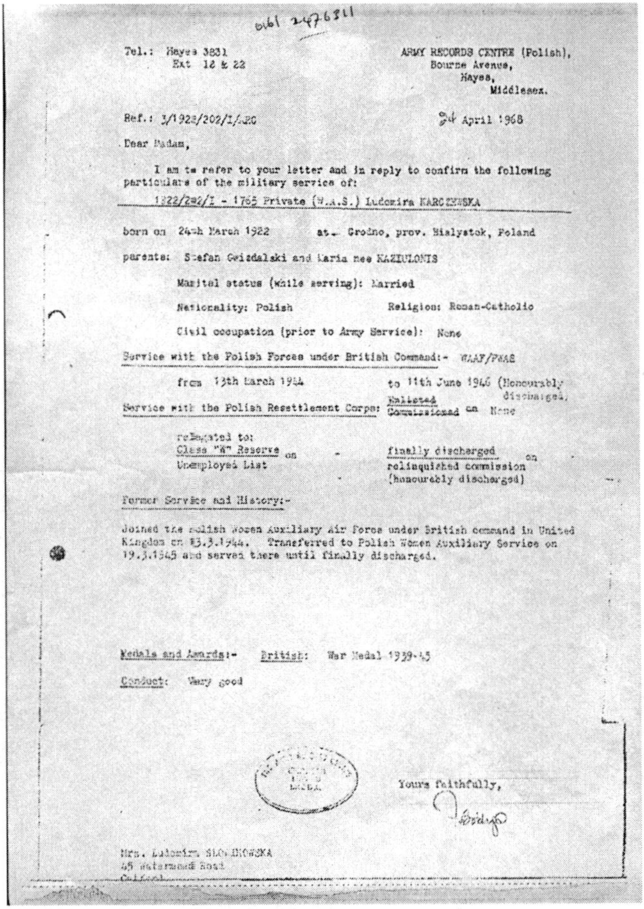

0161 2476311

Tel.: Hayes 3831
Ext 12 & 22

ARMY RECORDS CENTRE (Polish),
Bourne Avenue,
Hayes,
Middlesex.

Ref.: 3/1922/202/I/ARC

24 April 1968

Dear Madam,

I am to refer to your letter and in reply to confirm the following particulars of the military service of:

1922/202/I - 1765 Private (W.A.S.) Ludomira KARCZEWSKA

born on 24th March 1922 at Grodno, prov. Bialystok, Poland

parents: Stefan Gwizdalski and Maria nee KAZIULONIS

Marital status (while serving): Married

Nationality: Polish Religion: Roman-Catholic

Civil occupation (prior to Army Service): None

Service with the Polish Forces under British Command:- WAAF/PWAS

from 13th March 1944 to 11th June 1946 (Honourably discharged)

Service with the Polish Resettlement Corps: Enlisted / Commissioned on None

relegated to:
Class "W" Reserve / Unemployed List on -

finally discharged / relinquished commission (honourably discharged) on -

Former Service and History:-

Joined the Polish Women Auxiliary Air Force under British command in United Kingdom on 13.3.1944. Transferred to Polish Women Auxiliary Service on 19.3.1945 and served there until finally discharged.

Medals and Awards:- British: War Medal 1939-45

Conduct: Very good

Yours faithfully,

Mrs. Ludomira SLOWIKOWSKA
45 Watermead Road

Army Records Centre, Middlesex

St Catherine's House, Heathfield

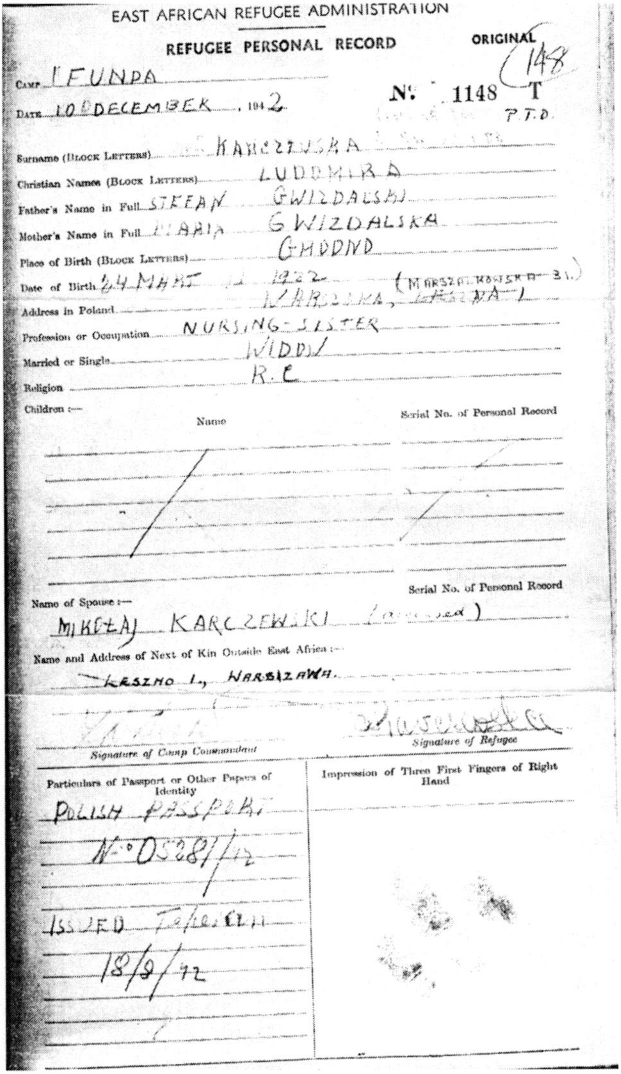

EAST AFRICAN REFUGEE ADMINISTRATION

REFUGEE PERSONAL RECORD

ORIGINAL 1148

Camp IFUNDA

Date 10 DECEMBER, 1942

No. 1148 T

P.T.O.

Surname (Block Letters) KARCZEWSKA

Christian Names (Block Letters) LUDOMIRA

Father's Name in Full STEFAN GWIZDALSKI

Mother's Name in Full MARIA GWIZDALSKA

Place of Birth (Block Letters) GRODNO

Date of Birth 24 MARZ 1922 (MARSZAŁKOWSKA 31.)

Address in Poland WARSZAWA, LESZNO 1

Profession or Occupation NURSING-SISTER

Married or Single WIDOW

Religion R.C.

Children :—

Name	Serial No. of Personal Record

Name of Spouse :— MIKOŁAJ KARCZEWSKI

Serial No. of Personal Record

Name and Address of Next of Kin Outside East Africa :— LESZNO 1, WARSZAWA.

Signature of Camp Commandant

Signature of Refugee

Particulars of Passport or Other Papers of Identity

POLISH PASSPORT
No 0528/42
ISSUED TEHERAN
18/9/42

Impression of Three First Fingers of Right Hand

East African Refugee Document

Ref. 3a (101)
28.1.46. Left to join W.A.A.F. in England.

POLISH INSTITUTE AND SIKORSKI MUSEUM
Archive Ref. No KOL. 320/17/148
Copyright: Polish Institute and Sikorski Museum

Document held at the Polish Institute and Sikorski Museum

Warszawa, Marszałkowska 31
Zarząd Miejski, Wydział Planowania
Miasta. 11.2.1939 r.
Sekcja Planowania, Referat Gabarytów.

31 Marszalkowska, Warsawa, 1939

The Grodno Oblast' Executive Committee
Department of Archives and Business Records
THE GRODNO OBLAST' STATE ARCHIVE SCIENTIFIC AUTHORITY
84 Dzerzhinsky Street, 23005 Grodno
Tel/Fax: (0152) 72-24-43, 77-04-92
Payment Acct. 3710000000733, Branch 400
Grodno District Office for ASB Belarus'bank, Code 752, UNN 500044112

Date: 4 July 2005
No.: 139

To: The Consular Department
Belarusian Ministry of Internal Affairs
Minsk

We are sending you herewith a request from Norwegian citizen Anna Karchevskaya-Williams and an archive certificate that Stefan Gvizdal'skii, born 1898, the son of Anton and Anna, lived with his wife Maria Gvizdal'skaya, born 1899, and daughter Lyutsiya (name as shown in documents), born 1922, in Grodno at 11 Ulitsa Grandichskaya. The house was registered in 1885.

No other information has been found in the archives on the Gvizdal'skii family.

Attached: 2 sheets

L. V. Kisyel' Deputy Archive Director
I. M. Voronko Head of Department

WE APLIN TRANSLATION SERVICES OF WHITEFRIARS LEWINS MEAD BRISTOL BS1 2NT DO CERTIFY THAT THE ATTACHED TRANSLATION IS TO THE BEST OF OUR KNOWLEDGE AND BELIEF AN ACCURATE RENDERING OF THE ORIGINAL DOCUMENT.

Signed:
26/11/07

The Grodno State Archives, July 2005

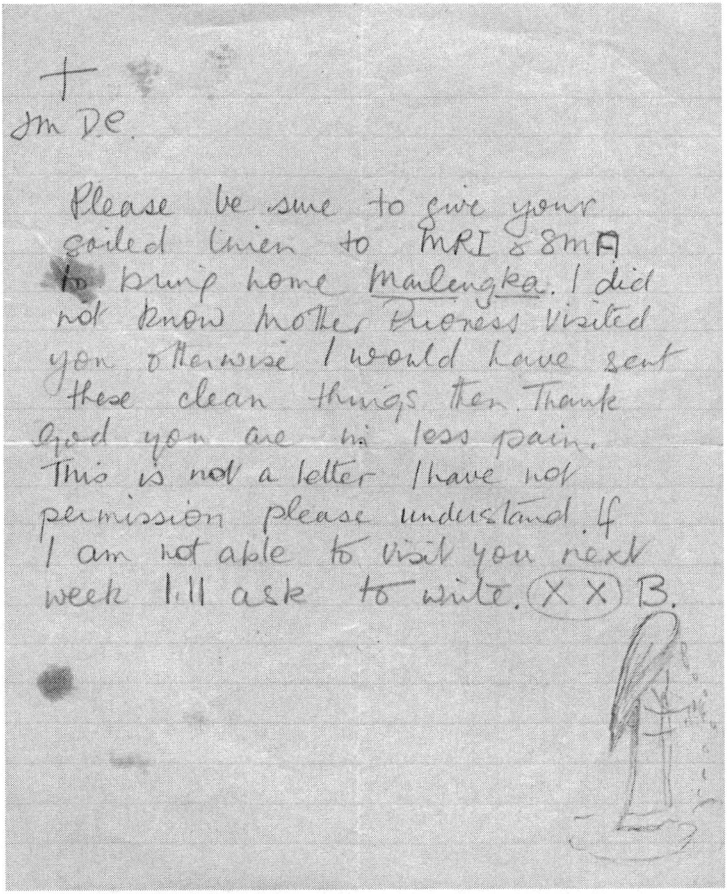

+

Jm DC.

Please be sure to give your soiled linen to MRI & 8MA to bring home Malengka. I did not know Mother Prioress visited you otherwise I would have sent these clean things then. Thank God you are in less pain. This is not a letter I have not permission please understand. If I am not able to visit you next week I'll ask to write. (X X) B.

Letter from Nursing Sister (not dated)

Mother on her wedding day, 1956, Brompton Church, Kensington

References

Borowski, Tadeusz *This Way to the Gas Ladies and Gentlemen*, Penguin, 1976.
Davies, Norman *God's Playground*, Oxford 2005.
Davies, Norman *Trail of Hope*, Osprey 2015.
Hoffman, Eva *After Such Knowledge*, Vintage 2005.
Kochanski, Halik *The Eagle Unbowed*, Penguin 2012.
Orr, Aileen *Wojtek the Bear*, Birlinn 2012.
The Poles in Great Britain 1971 The Polish Ex-Combatants Association and the British Council for Aid to Refugees.